THEN & NOW

MILTON

This southward view of Randolph Avenue in 1949 shows the intersection known as Cohan's Corner, the junction of Pleasant Street (left) and Reedsdale Road. The intersection was named in honor of Cornelius and Dermis C. Cohan, who kept a corner variety store, later a pharmacy, on the left-hand side. On the right is the old St. Elizabeth's Roman Catholic Church, which was demolished after the present English Gothic church was built in 1964 on the opposite corner. (Courtesy of the Milton Historical Society.)

THEN & NOW

MILTON

Anthony Mitchell Sammarco

ARCADIA PUBLISHING

ISBN 978-0-7385-3695-8

Published by Arcadia Publishing,
Charleston, South Carolina

Printed in the United States of America

Library of Congress Catalog Card Number: 2004110650

For all general information, contact Arcadia Publishing:
Telephone 843-853-2070
Fax 843-853-0044
E-mail sales@arcadiapublishing.com
For customer service and orders:
Toll-free 1-888-313-2665

Visit us on the Internet at www.arcadiapublishing.com

In honor of the centennial of the Milton Historical Society, 1904–2004.

Musicians sit on the flag-bedecked flatbed of a truck as they serenade Milton residents wishing to purchase bonds during World War I. The placard reads, "Who Supports the Soldiers & Sailors? You Do. When you buy a Liberty Bond." The truck is stopped in front of the Blue Hill National Bank, now the site of Jack Conway Real Estate, in the Associates Building at the corner of Adams and Wharf Streets in Milton Village. (Courtesy of the Milton Historical Society.)

Contents

ACKNOWLEDGMENTS

I would like to thank the following for their assistance, either directly or indirectly, in writing this book: Donald Agnetta; Anthony Bognanno; the Boston Athenaeum, Sally Pierce, Print Room; Helen G. Buchanan; the late Paul G. Buchanan; Nicholas S. F. Carter; Frank Cheney; Elise Ciregna; Edith G. Clifford, co-president of the Milton Historical Society; Edith Cunningham Crocker; John and Maritta Manning Cronin; Martha T. Curtis; Elizabeth Curtiss; Annie Davis; Rupert Davis; Pat Desmond, editor at the *Milton Times;* Dexter; Brian Doherty; Kevin Donahue; Olivia Dybing; Joan Estelle Evans; William P. Fall; First Parish in Milton, Unitarian; Robert M. Fitzgerald, co-president of the Milton Historical Society; Christine Sullivan, director of the Captain Forbes House Museum; Andrea and Marvin Gordon; Edward W. Gordon; Dan Haacker; Meredith Hall; Helen Hannon; Peter Hanson and Joan Halpert; Tiffany Howe, my publisher; Nadine A. Leary; the late William Leary; Judith McGillicuddy; Harriet Manning; the Milton Fire Department; the Milton Historical Society; the Milton Police Department and chief Kevin Mearn; Philip McNulty, director of the Milton Public Library; Joseph O'Neill; Evelyn O' Sullivan; Ellen Ochs; Michael Monti Parise; Fran Perkins; Jeannette L. Peverly; Linda M. Pirie; Eva Proctor; Lilian M. S. Randall; Margaret S. Recanzone; Bernadette C. Richards; Perry Russell; Anthony and Mary Mitchell Sammarco; the late Warren Craig Scott; Therese Desmond-Sills; Jeanne Sutton; Anne and George Thompson; Carolyn D. Thornton; John Avery Tucker; Ruth Tucker; Ann and Thomas Walsh; Richard H. Walwood; Frances K. Westerbeke; and the late Norman Whiting.

I wish to extend special thanks to Charlie Rosenberg for his exceptional work in taking the contemporary photographs.

A portion of the royalties from the sale of this book will benefit the Milton Historical Society.

INTRODUCTION

Milton was settled in 1640 by Puritans who began the settlement of Massachusetts Bay Colony in 1630. Originally a part of the town of Dorchester, Milton was incorporated as an independent town in 1662 and remains as such today, although it borders the burgeoning city of Boston on the north along the Neponset River. For well over two centuries after its founding, Milton remained a primarily agrarian community with farms and open lands, as well as industrial activity along the Neponset River at Milton Village; it included a gristmill, a gunpowder mill, a paper mill, and a chocolate mill—all thought to be among the first of their kind in New England. After the Civil War, however, Milton's population began to rapidly increase due to the convenience of the Milton and Dorchester branch of the Old Colony Railroad, which provided railway access to Boston with a depot at Mattapan Square and passenger stations at Central Avenue and Milton Village. Today, the former railroad line is perpetuated by the surface trolley connecting Ashmont Station and Mattapan Square and has stations on both the Dorchester and Milton sides of the river. A horse-drawn streetcar began running in 1856 from the Lower Mills to downtown Boston via Dorchester Avenue, so the ease of transportation allowed people of all walks of life to live in Milton but to commute to the city for employment.

In the May 12, 1883, edition of the *Milton News,* there appeared an editorial that is considered startlingly prophetic as to the rampant development that would occur in the town over the next century. It said, "Milton is so conveniently located near Boston that its growth as a dwelling place for people carrying on business in the metropolis is assured beyond a doubt. The only drawback to a rapid growth is the manifest desire of many land owners to keep their property out of the market and thereby preserve the antiquity of its topography. . . . A truly good man will not monopolize all the eligible real estate for his own gratification alone, it will be either for the purpose of doing some good, real or imaginary to the community or town, or a combination of circumstances may draw him to withhold it for a better end."

By the mid-19th century, Milton was no longer a rural farming town. Located just seven miles from the Massachusetts State House, the town had thriving industrial concerns along the Neponset River and businesses in Milton Village and East Milton. The Granite Railway Company had, since its inception in 1826, provided quarried granite for a multitude of purposes and could boast of being the first railway in the United States. From what was once a primarily agrarian community, Milton had by 1865 attracted numerous families who purchased the former farms and open lands to create gentlemen's estates that varied in size from a few acres to over 100. These new families, some of which had connections to Milton through birth or marriage, created a network of families and friends that sought to retain the rural character of Milton, but by the early 20th century, rampant development was taking place on all sides—in Dorchester, Mattapan, and Hyde Park on the north and in Quincy on the south. The population increased steadily, and by the turn of the century, Milton had become an affluent and desirable town with proximity to the city.

After World War I, many of the farms and large estates were to be subdivided and developed for residential housing. Among these great estates was the Cunningham estate on Edge Hill Road. It was sold in 1904 to the trustees of the Mary Cunningham Trust to become a park for the future benefit of Milton residents, a role it still plays a century after it was created. The estate was preserved virtually intact, with the mansion later being used as the Milton Convalescent Home and Hospital. Many large estates were systematically developed throughout the town, with house lots being laid out. Among them were, on Milton Hill, Brookmount (the Nathaniel Safford estate), Fredonia (the John Murray Forbes estate), and Eastover (the Ernest Bowdith estate). In East Milton were Carmarthen (the Charles Davis estate), Indian Hollow (the Francis J. O. Alsop estate), and Overlook (the David Clark estate). In the western areas were the enormous Eustis and Hemenway estates, as well as the Pines (the Hunt-Salter estate, now Curry College), Fair Oaks (the Wallace L. Pierce estate), Brushwood (the Amor Hollingsworth estate), and the estate of Henry A. Whitney. Smaller estates—including Smallsizes, which became Meredith Circle; Three Pines, which became Fairfax Street; and the massive Home Farm, which was developed as Indian Cliffs—meant that these once placid estates would all be developed with new streets and house lots for upscale residences. Pine Tree Brook (the more than 100-acre Rotch-Lamb estate at Blue Hills Parkway and Canton Avenue) survived until the 1970s. It was then sold by the heirs and is now HOME Inc., an attractive and affordable senior residential development, which has ensured that senior residents will remain a part of the community.

In the 20th century, tremendous changes took place in Milton. As Edward Pierce Hamilton said, by 1929, "the whole character and aspect of our town [changed] in a very great increase in population." In some instances, areas were changed beyond recognition, while others had infill development that augmented the area usage with both residential and commercial development. With the laying out of the Southeast Expressway through Milton in the 1950s, a wide swath was cut through East Milton, virtually dividing the area with a suppressed roadbed, ironically, along the path of the Granite Railway, the first railroad in the United States. The railway was laid out in 1826 to transport quarried granite to be used in the building of the Bunker Hill Monument in Charlestown, Massachusetts. Granite Avenue, quite appropriately named, paralleled the new highway, and the area was reconfigured over the next few decades. Other areas of the town, such as Brush Hill, Scots Woods, and upper Canton Avenue, remained largely intact, with minor infilling of residences, thereby preserving its semirural charm.

In this book, I have tried to chronicle, in a visual format, the tremendous changes that took place in Milton in the last century. With the able assistance of Charlie Rosenberg, who worked on three previous books with me in 2003, the present-day photographs show the poignancy of the older images and how important local preservation is to retain the salient features so valued to its history. The book begins with a chapter on town-related buildings, followed by chapters on schools and places of worship. The rest of the book is divided by geographic sections. In some cases, exact modern-day photographs were impossible. Unfortunately, due to space constraints, I was able to include only a small photographic sampling of the town's developmental history; I beg your indulgence in any oversight or omission.

Chapter 1
THE TOWN OF MILTON

The Milton Town Hall was built in 1878 on Canton Avenue between the First Parish in Milton, Unitarian and the First Congregational Church. Designed by the noted architectural firm of Hartwell and Tilden, it was a red-brick and granite hall with an asymmetrical tower and a Romanesque Revival entrance. Today, the Lira Bandstand is on the site of the old town hall. The bandstand was built in 1990 through the generosity of Baron Hugo Lira, "King of the Totem Pole Ballroom," in memory of his wife, Edith Hamilton Lira. (Courtesy of the Milton Historical Society, Whiting collection.)

Children leave the First Parish Church, Unitarian in 1949 to attend their own services in the Children's Church, a former private school built in 1844. In 1937, it was moved from the estate of John Murray Forbes on Adams Street and converted to a place where Sunday school was held. Remodeled by Eliot T. Putnam of Putnam and Cox, it became known as the Little Church where "the young folk of the parish will worship." The First Parish Church, Unitarian was founded in 1678, and this church, the fourth meetinghouse, was built in 1787. (Courtesy of the Milton Public Library.)

The first town hall was a small, one-story Greek Revival building built in 1837 between the two churches on Academy Hill. The building was very simple, having only corner pilasters and a pedimented façade, and town meetings were held here for 41 years. A corner of the First Parish in Milton, Unitarian, the oldest church in Milton, can be seen on the left. The site was later occupied by the Hartwell and Tilden–designed Milton Town Hall and is now the site of the Lira Bandstand. (Courtesy of First Parish in Milton, Unitarian.)

The town hall, seen in 1959, was a radically different form of architecture from the two white churches that flanked it. Controversy arose in the 1960s when the town decided to replace the structure with a new town hall. The pros and cons were seriously debated at town meetings, and the building was eventually demolished, making way for the new town hall to be built to the rear. The present hall was designed by Richard C. Stauffer and Associates and built in 1970. The Lira Bandstand is located on the site of the original town hall. (Author's collection.)

The Central Fire Station was built in 1888 by J. H. Burt and Company directly behind town hall on the appropriately named Engine Street. An impressive vernacular Colonial Revival red-brick and granite-lintel building, the station also boasted a Palladian window in the frontal gable and an asymmetrical corner tower. It had a chemical engine and was equipped with a quick hitching harness for a pair of horses to pull the engine. Today, the tower has been shortened, and a two-bay addition for larger fire engines was added to the far left. (Author's collection.)

The Chemical Engine No. 1 was built in 1884 by J. H. Burt and Company. The building resolved the great concern of town residents as to where the first chemical engine purchased by the town that year would be housed. A simple, two-story, red-brick and granite-lintel building, it was used by the fire department for many years. Today, the building is occupied by the Milton Wire Department, and the Milton Firefighters Memorial Archives, maintained by the Milton Fire Department Auxiliary, are located on the second floor. Seen in front of the building are Dave Staunton and Mike Murphy. (Above, courtesy of the Milton Public Library; left, courtesy of Brian Doherty.)

Hose No. 2 was a wood engine house in East Milton between Adams Street and Granite Avenue (originally known as Willard Street from Adams Street to the Quincy line). Members of the Milton Fire Department pose in 1915 with a horse-drawn vehicle in front of the engine house. The present East Milton Fire Station, built in 1952, is a red-brick and cement two-bay structure. Seen in front are firefighters Dave Staunton and Mike Murphy. (Below, courtesy of the Milton Public Library; right, courtesy of Brian Doherty.)

The Milton Public Library was designed by the noted architectural firm of Shepley, Rutan, and Coolidge and opened in 1904 at the corner of Canton Avenue and Reedsdale Road. Founded in 1871, the library was originally located in Milton Village in the Baker Building and, later, in the Associates Building. However, the growing population created a need for a larger and more centrally located building. The new structure was an impressive Beaux Arts–style building of brick and sandstone, with twin monumental Ionic columns flanking the entrance and a parapet surmounted by the seal of the town. (Courtesy of the Milton Public Library.)

Members of the Milton Police Department pose in front of police headquarters *c.* 1905. The red-brick and granite-linteled Milton Lockup, as it was known, was built in 1884 by J. H. Burt and Company at the town landing on Wharf Street in Milton Village. The police force was officially established in 1890, with Maurice Pierce serving as superintendent. Today, the former police station is the headquarters of the Milton Yacht Club. (Courtesy of the Milton Historical Society.)

The second police headquarters was located on Central Avenue at Burke Square. It was originally built in 1890 by Edwin T. Ruggles as the generator station of the Milton Light and Power Company building, later the Edison Illuminating Lighting Company. The building was purchased in 1905, and its use as police quarters ran from 1906 until 1973, when the present headquarters on Highland Street was built. The original structure was then demolished, and a small parking lot was created for shoppers patronizing Central Avenue businesses. (Courtesy of Nadine Leary.)

The first Milton High School was built by William B. Crehore in 1807. It was originally constructed as Academy House, a part of Milton Academy on Academy Hill, the area of Milton Centre located near the town hall and fire station. The schoolhouse was a large, two-story Federal building with an octagonal cupola. The academy suspended its charter in 1866, so the building was leased to the town of Milton until 1885, when a new high school was designed and built by Rotch and Tilden on the site of the old academy building. (Courtesy of Marvin and Andrea Gordon.)

Chapter 2
MILTON PUBLIC SCHOOLS

The Old West School, often referred to as the Old Brick, was built in 1812 at the corner of Blue Hill Avenue and Atherton Street. Seen here *c.* 1865, the schoolchildren stand in front. The school was demolished in 1870, when the Sumner School, named for settler William Sumner (1604–1698) was built on the site. Today, Coulter Landscaping and Greenhouses occupies the site of the school, and the Atherton Fire Station is on the right. (Courtesy of the Milton Historical Society, Baxter collection.)

The Old East School was built in 1852 on Adams Street, near Squantum Street in East Milton. The building was greatly enlarged in 1877. Seen here in 1860, students in the primary, intermediate, and grammar classes stand in front of the school and also sit in the second-floor windows for the photographer. The building was demolished in 1894, and the site is now adjacent to the campus of St. Agatha's Roman Catholic Church. (Courtesy of the Milton Historical Society, Baxter collection.)

The Houghton School was located on Hillside Street in the Scots Woods section of town and was the successor to the Scots Woods School. It was named for Ralph Houghton (1623–1705), an early settler for whom Houghton's Pond was also named. A large, two-story schoolhouse, it served the needs of students on the south side of town until 1922, when it was closed. Today, 322 Hillside Street, a modern house, stands on the foundations of the former school. (Courtesy of the Milton Historical Society.)

The Wadsworth School, formerly the Pleasant Street School, was built in 1879. It replaced the earlier school built in 1853, located at the corner of Pleasant and Gun Hill Streets. The school was in an area referred to as New State because many townspeople in the 19th century thought some of the residents were loafers who should form a new state of their own. The Wadsworth School was a large Italianate schoolhouse, and it had an addition on the rear. Teachers pose on the front steps for this *c.* 1885 photograph. (Courtesy of the Milton Historical Society.)

Milton High School, built in 1885, was designed by the noted architectural firm of Rotch and Tilden. A large addition was added in 1895 by architect Bradford O. Hamilton (1856–1944). The school was built behind the Milton Town Hall on the site of the old academy building and was an impressive Romanesque Revival brick school. In 1917, it became known as the Vose School and was used as an elementary school until its demolition in 1956. The Central Fire House can be seen on the right. (Courtesy of Nadine Leary.)

The Vose School was designed by Kilham and Hopkins and built in 1909 at the junction of Brook Road and Central Avenue. In 1917, the school became Milton High School and was greatly enlarged with the addition of a science wing, gymnasium, assembly hall, and locker rooms. Today, the former Milton High School is undergoing tremendous changes with new additions and renovations by Drummey Rosane Anderson Inc. and will be known as the Pierce Middle School. (Author's collection.)

The Thacher School was an impressive Shingle-style school built in 1890 on Walnut Avenue. It was named for Rev. Peter Thacher (1651–1727), the first minister of the Milton Meetinghouse. During World War II, the former school was the headquarters of the Milton chapter of the American Red Cross and later housed the town engineer and the water department. Today, it is the site of the Milton Council on Aging. (Courtesy of Nadine Leary.)

The Belcher School was a large wood Colonial Revival school on Church Street, near Church Place. Built in 1894, it was named for the royal governor, Jonathan Belcher (1681–1757), whose summer house was on Adams Street. Belcher served as governor from 1729 to 1741, after which he was appointed governor of New Jersey in 1747. There he founded the College of New Jersey, later renamed Princeton University. Today, the site of the school is a cul-de-sac off Church Street with modern houses. (Courtesy of Nadine Leary.)

The Pierce Elementary School was designed as a concrete-and-brick school by Adden, Parker, Clinch, and Crimp and built in 1952 on Gile Road. It was named for Charles Sumner Pierce, a prominent banker and town meeting moderator. In 1958, a junior high school was added, which became the only junior high school in Milton. Today, the school is being replaced by a more modern structure by Drummey Rosane Anderson Inc. and will be used as Milton High School. (Courtesy of the Milton Historical Society, Hamilton collection.)

Chapter 3
PLACES OF WORSHIP

Founded in 1678, the First Parish in Milton, Unitarian is the oldest congregation in town. The first settled minister was Rev. Peter Thacher. The fourth meetinghouse, seen in this photograph, was built in 1787 and was moved in 1835 to face Canton Avenue. (Courtesy of the Milton Historical Society, Whiting collection.)

The First Congregational Church was founded in 1834 as the result of a theological disagreement concerning the popular Unitarian belief that had been embraced by the town. Those seeking Orthodox Congregationalism withdrew and built their church on the opposite end of the town common. In 1949, Arland A. Dirlam remodeled and enlarged the church with the addition of a parish house and removal of the horse sheds in the rear. Recently the church built a large addition in the rear known as the Centre School. (Courtesy of the Milton Public Library.)

The Second Congregational (now known as the East Congregational) Church was built in 1846 at 577 Adams Street in East Milton to serve the needs of those moving to the area to work in the granite industry. A large Italianate church, it was set along a residential street, and late–Greek Revival houses can be seen flanking it on Adams Street. From 1950 to the early 1980s, it was used as the Elks Club, and today the former church has been converted to condominiums. A new church was designed by Arland A. Dirlam and built in 1950 diagonally across the street. To the left is the Bates House, at 583–585 Adams Street, and on the right is the Orin Bates House, at 569–571 Adams Street. (Courtesy of the Milton Historical Society.)

St. Michael's Church was designed by Ralph Lincoln Emerson (1868–1899) and built in 1898 at 112 Randolph Avenue near Milton Village. A late–Gothic Revival design with random ashlar stone and an asymmetrical tower, it is today set on well-landscaped grounds. Emerson graduated from Harvard in 1891 and studied architecture with his father, William Ralph Emerson. His design for the church included a nave and small chancel. In 1916, Ralph Adams Cram enlarged the chancel, along with the Tudor Revival parish house, with a combination of timbering and stucco that emulated medieval wattle and daub. (Courtesy of the Milton Historical Society, Whiting collection.)

The Church of Our Savior in East Milton was designed by William Ralph Emerson (1833–1917) and built in 1903 at the corner of Adams and Babcock Streets. A small church in the English Gothic Perpendicular style, it has the feeling of a small English parish church. It was enlarged in 1924 with an additional bay and accommodations for a choir and stalls. Once under the direction of St. Michael's Church as a mission church beginning in 1897, it became a mission of the Diocese of Massachusetts in 1923. (Courtesy of Nadine Leary.)

The First Baptist Church was built in 1893 on Edge Hill Road as a large Shingle-style church with an impressive tower on the right. The church was damaged in the hurricane of 1938, and the tower was rebuilt and lowered. Later, the façade was stuccoed and applied with a combination of permastone and half-timbering, which dramatically altered the exterior. The church is adjacent to the East Milton Library. (Courtesy of the Milton Historical Society, Whiting collection.)

The Mattapan Baptist Church was designed by George Hunt Ingraham, a Milton architect, and built in 1901 at the corner of the Blue Hills Parkway and Eliot Street. A small wood-framed chapel, it was greatly enlarged in 1932 by the Boston architectural firm of Woodbury and Stuart. (Author's collection.)

St. Agatha's Church was founded in 1922 as an independent parish with Fr. Eugene A. Carney as first pastor. A small stone chapel was erected in 1917 as a mission of St. Gregory's Church in Dorchester to serve the Catholics of East Milton. The present church was designed as an impressive Modern Gothic design by Milton architect Alexander J. Scholtes (1880–1948). It was built in 1935 to serve the Roman Catholics of the eastern section of Milton and included a parochial school designed by Joseph McGann. (Author's collection.)

St. Elizabeth's Church was established in 1946 to alleviate the overcrowded Roman Catholic parishes in town. Fr. Joseph J. Keenan served as the first pastor. The parishioners first worshiped in a former army chapel brought from Camp Miles Standish, which was dedicated as a memorial to those who served in the armed forces. The simple chapel was adjacent to the old Joseph Howe House, built *c.* 1830 of granite by a man associated with the granite industry. The present St. Elizabeth's Church was designed by John M. Gray and Company and built in 1964 on the opposite corner. (Courtesy of Anne and George Thompson.)

Temple Shalom was founded in 1943 and built at 180 Blue Hill Avenue and was originally known as the Milton Hebrew Center. Temple Shalom had been founded to serve the needs of conservative Jews in Milton, some of whom had once worshiped in the many synagogues in Dorchester and Roxbury. Today, Temple Shalom has been expanded to serve a growing congregation that encompasses many in "an egalitarian, multigenerational congregation that welcomes diversity, spirituality and community." (Courtesy of the Milton Public Library.)

Chapter 4
Milton Village

Milton Village was a busy area, as this 1936 photograph shows. The Suffolk Resolves House and the Associates Building are seen on the east side of Adams Street. The Suffolk Resolves House, once home to Daniel and Rachel Smith Vose, was moved in 1950 to its present location at 1370 Canton Avenue, where it is currently the headquarters of the Milton Historical Society. The Associates Building was designed by the noted Boston architectural firm of Rotch and Tilden and built in 1882 with commercial space along the first floor, professional offices above that, and Associates Hall on the third floor. The massive elm tree in the foreground, planted in 1785, was being removed due to Dutch elm disease. (Courtesy of the Milton Historical Society, Baxter collection.)

The Vose House became known as the Suffolk Resolves House when delegates met in 1774 to sign a petition of grievances that became known as the Suffolk Resolves. They were taken by Paul Revere via horseback to the Continental Congress in Philadelphia. For many years, the former residence became used for commercial stores, including a book drop for the library upstairs, until it was condemned and moved in 1950. The Milton Savings Bank built its headquarters on the site in 1950, and Citizens Bank occupies the location today. (Courtesy of the Milton Historical Society.)

The Crehore House was the home and shop of Benjamin Crehore, a noted inventor and manufacturer of pianofortes and bas viols. He reputedly made the first American-manufactured pianoforte, set in a mahogany case manufactured by one of the fine cabinetmakers in the village. Today, the Milton Professional Building, formerly Preston's Market, is on the site of the shop. On the right is the former Fenno House, built *c.* 1765. (Author's collection.)

The house of Dr. Jonathan Ware was located in Milton Village, adjacent to the Neponset River and near his chocolate mill. A large house, it became the home of H. Clifford Gallagher, president of the Baker Chocolate Company. The wood mill on the far left was built in 1728 for Jeremiah Smith, who produced paper here. Ware's Chocolate Mill occupied the space from 1843 to 1881. The Ware-Gallagher House was replaced in 1892 by Baker Chocolate's circular storage warehouses, which are now used by the Extra Space Storage Company. (Courtesy of the Milton Public Library.)

The former Miss Miller's Female Seminary, an academy for young ladies, was an impressive Greek Revival, Ionic-colonnaded building built in 1839 overlooking the Neponset River. In 1885, it became the noted Milton Hill House, a genteel boardinghouse operated by George A. Nickerson for the Whitney family. Many Milton families patronized the house before or after closing their summer houses, and there were also numerous loyal boarders who stayed there. Today, the Milton Hill House is a modern concrete and red-brick apartment building. (Author's collection.)

The Rising Sun Tavern was a noted inn located on Canton Avenue between High and Adams Streets. Stagecoaches traveling to and from Boston changed horses here while passengers refreshed themselves with warm food and potent libations before they resumed their journey. Today, the Chapman, Cole, and Gleason Funeral House occupies the site. (Courtesy of the Milton Historical Society, Whiting collection.)

The Baker Building was erected by Edmund J. Baker on Adams Street. It later moved to Wharf Street, and in 1871 it became the first site of the Milton Public Library. After 1904, when the present Milton Public Library was opened, this building was moved across Adams Street and remodeled. It is now the Therese Marie Photo Studio. (Courtesy of the Milton Public Library.)

Maj. Phineas Paine built this house *c.* 1805 on Adams Street in Milton Village, which was a true mill village with residences, stores, and craftsmen shops all located in the area. On the left is a corner of the Fenno House, now 71 Adams Street, and on the right is Lemuel Crossman's livery stable, which burned in 1953. The site of the Paine House became a Jenney gas station in the 1950s, and today it is a drive-through Citizens Bank. (Courtesy of the Milton Historical Society.)

The Samuel Gannett store, seen from Eliot Street in 1910, was a successful grain, flour, hay, and straw store on Adams Street. The five-bay building was built in 1793 by John Lille and used as his store. On the right is Nathan C. Martin's store (built in 1827), which was later used as the Milton Fruit Store. Joseph J. Simonetti (1882–1972) kept the store from 1913 until the 1940s. Today, the sidewalk drops off here, and the storage warehouses can be seen in the distance. (Courtesy of the Milton Historical Society, Baxter collection.)

The Milton station of the Dorchester and Milton branch of the Old Colony Railroad had a long, one-story waiting room and ticket office located below the buildings along Adams Street. It could be reached via a staircase or by Wharf Street. After 1929, this became the Milton stop on the surface trolley connecting Ashmont Station and Mattapan. Notice the Baker Mill, designed by Winslow and Wetherell and built in 1895, on the left and the Pierce Mill, designed by Nathaniel J. Bradlee and built in 1872, on the right of the Baker Chocolate Company. (Courtesy of Nadine Leary.)

Algerine Corner is the junction of Centre, Pleasant, and Adams Streets. Its charm was captured in an 1851 watercolor by noted architect and artist Edward Clarke Cabot. The lot, which was owned by Edward Hutchinson Robbins, was often the victim of thievery, as young men pilfered firewood during the period of the early 19th century, when local ships were having trouble with Algerian pirates. Robbins called the wood poachers a "set of Algerines," and the name stuck, though the town once tried renaming the area Union Square following the Civil War. (Courtesy of the Boston Athenaeum.)

Chapter 5
MILTON HILL

The Gooch-Churchill House was built by Col. Joseph Gooch *c.* 1740 at 233 Adams Street, possibly the site of the first meetinghouse in Milton. Later, Asaph Churchill (1765–1841) lived here, and Churchill's Lane, once known as Middle Street, perpetuates his name. Churchill was an attorney, a member of the legislature, and a man of "independent disposition and strong individuality." (Courtesy of the Milton Historical Society, Sutermeister collection.)

The Holbrook-Cunningham House was built in 1801 by Amos Holbrook (1754–1842), a noted physician who was among the first in the country to inoculate patients for smallpox at the crest of Milton Hill. The house was later the home of Mary Abbot Forbes Cunningham (1814–1904), widow of Rev. Francis Cunningham, whose considerable fortune was left to three trustees to be used for the benefit the residents of Milton. The trustees established a fund, and their successors have since operated Cunningham Park, on Edge Hill Road, through the income from her trust. (Courtesy of the Forbes House Museum.)

Isaiah Rogers was commissioned to build a mansion for Margaret Perkins Forbes, widow of Ralph Forbes (1773–1824), on the crest of Milton Hill. Built in 1834, it is an impressive Greek Revival house that had an octagonal oculus that overlooked Boston and the harbor. Enlarged in 1873 by the noted architectural firm of Peabody and Stearns, the Castle, as the family referred to it, became the Captain Forbes House Museum following the death of Mary Bowditch Forbes. (Courtesy of the Forbes House Museum.)

The Twin Cottage was built by John Murray Forbes as his first residence and got its name because it had the appearance of two houses joined together. Built at 240 Adams Street, opposite Dudley Lane, the house was later occupied by his son J. Murray Forbes and later leased to R. Dudley Peters. The house was demolished in 1937. (Courtesy of the Milton Historical Society.)

Fredonia was designed by noted architects Edward Clark Cabot and Eliot Cabot as the mansion of John Murray Forbes and Sarah Swain Hathaway Forbes. A massive red-brick Italianate house, it was set on a 28-acre estate and survived until the house was destroyed by a fire in 1949. Streets such as Milton Hill Road and Forbes Road were laid out through the estate and small ranch houses were built on the once bucolic estate. (Courtesy of the Forbes House Museum.)

The Ware Cottage was built by John Pope in 1844 for Mary Pickard Ware, a widow who moved from Cambridge, where she kept a private school, to Milton after an invitation of John Murray Forbes. Her husband had been a noted Unitarian minister, and she raised her remarkable children here. Among them were Emma Forbes Ware, Harriet Ware, and William R. Ware. She kept a school for the Forbes children and relations on the estate. In 1920, the house was demolished, and a new Colonial Revival mansion (designed by Putnam and Cox) was built for financier Malcolm Ware, a nephew. (Courtesy of the Milton Historical Society, Sutermeister collection.)

The Cary Mansion was a large Italianate house built by Edward Montague Cary (1828–1888) and Alice Hathaway Forbes Cary on the southeastern slope of Milton Hill. The Carys owned 10 acres that were developed by the Cary Hill Realty Company and the John J. Gallagher and Associates after Mrs. Cary's death in 1917. Cabot Road and Cary Avenue were laid out with large one-family houses built in the subdivision. (Courtesy of the Forbes House Museum.)

The Russell-Rivers House was built in 1871 on the foundation of Unquety, the house of royal governor Thomas Hutchinson (1711–1780), on Milton Hill. A large Shingle-style Victorian mansion, it was located at the corner of Adams and Hutchinson Streets and was set on a vast estate that extended back toward Randolph Avenue. The Russell-Rivers family lived here until the 1930s, and during World War II, the house served as the headquarters of the Milton chapter of the American Red Cross. It was demolished, and new houses were built in the early 1950s; a barn was remodeled into 15 Hutchinson Street. (Courtesy of the Milton Historical Society.)

The Russell-Rivers estate had a large farmhouse that was later remodeled as a private residence for George R. R. Rivers (1853–1900) at 4 Hutchinson Street. Dating from 1743, it was a part of the large estate of Gov. Thomas Hutchinson and was remodeled and enlarged in the 19th century. The house had Gothic Revival details, but the Colonial Revival addition had interesting touches, such as an octagonal bay, a columned porch, balustrades, and a large addition. (Courtesy of the Milton Public Library.)

Chapter 6

Along Canton Avenue

The blacksmith shop shown below was located on Canton Avenue facing Mattapan Street (now the Blue Hills Parkway) at an area once referred to as Pine Tree Crossing. Operated by E. Blackman, the shop provided horseshoeing and carriage works. In this *c.* 1895 photograph, two carriages flank the entrance to the shop, while a carriage wheel pokes out of the loft door above. These blacksmith shops were a once common business in almost every New England town. The smith made horseshoes and shod horses, working with metal of all purposes and doing repair work. Today, this is the area of the Citgo gas station at Canton Avenue. (Courtesy of the Milton Public Library.)

The town pound was laid out in 1774 on Canton Avenue, opposite Holmes Lane, as the fourth pound in Milton's history. Cattle left roaming in fields were placed in a four-foot-tall stone enclosure. On the left is 637–635 Canton Avenue, a Victorian duplex, and on the right is Elm Street, which was laid out and named for a massive elm on the corner. (Courtesy of the Milton Historical Society, Baxter collection.)

The Gulliver Elm was a majestic tree that stood on Canton Avenue at the corner of Elm Street. The tree, with a 14-foot 4-inch trunk, was thought so important that it was deeded in 1833 to Isaac Gulliver by the First Congregational Church for future preservation and "perpetual exemption from molestation." In the distance can be seen Elm Street, which was a dirt road in 1905. It was later developed by Anthony V. Taurasi, and houses on the street were sold under the Federal Housing Association Plan in the late 1930s. Gulliver Street was also named in honor of the massive tree. (Courtesy of the Milton Historical Society.)

The small wood-framed cottage seen on the right was located at 720 Canton Avenue, otherwise known as the Home Farm, the vast estate of Henry Surgis Russell (1838–1905) and Mary Hathaway Forbes Russell. Following James Savage Russell's death in 1951, the estate was developed through the 1960s as Indian Cliffs, an upscale neighborhood. Modern houses have been built along Canton Avenue on this site. (Courtesy of Nadine Leary.)

Pine Tree Brook was the estate of Benjamin Smith Rotch (1817–1882), a wealthy merchant who also kept a townhouse in the Back Bay of Boston. The 100-acre estate, where he raised Jersey cattle, and its Italianate mansion were later inherited by his daughter Annie Lawrence Rotch Lamb, and her daughters Aimee and Rosamond Lamb, who used it as a spring and fall house as they summered in Maine. The property was sold by the Lamb Sisters to the town in the 1970s and developed as HOME Inc. (Courtesy of the Boston Athenaeum, Print Room.)

The Russell Mansion was a large house designed by William Ralph Emerson and built as the showplace of the Home Farm, the 300-acre estate that was landscaped by the Olmstead Associates, and horse stud of Henry Sturgis and Mary Forbes Russell. The horse stud was where noted racehorses Fearnaught and Dreadnaught were bred, and hundreds of horses were stabled here at the beginning of the 20th century. Seen standing on the entrance porch *c.* 1948 are James Savage Russell (1864–1951) and his second wife, Madeline Brewer Whitney Russell (1891–1977). (Courtesy of Perry Russell.)

Looking east on Canton Avenue at Sumner Street *c.* 1950, a corner of the Rotch-Lamb estate can be seen on the far left of the photograph. The open land on the right was developed in the 1970s by Fitzgerald Corporation as the Quisset Brook condominium complex, designed by Steffian-Bradley Associates of Boston. The area has since seen many new houses built in the last five decades. (Courtesy of the Milton Historical Society, Hamilton collection.)

The Blue Hill Market was a general store operated by H. B. Tucker at 959 Canton Avenue, opposite Harland Street. Built in 1850 by Stillman L. Tucker, the market was not just a place where staple groceries could be obtained, but also a stop of the Blue Hill and Boston Express, as well as home of the Blue Hill post office. To the right of the photograph are the canvas-covered horse-drawn wagons that the market used to deliver orders throughout the area. Today, the former market has been converted to a private residence. (Courtesy of the Milton Historical Society, Baxter collection.)

The Ebenezer Tucker House was built in 1707 on Canton Avenue. A five-bay second-period house with a center chimney, it represents an early example of domestic architecture in Milton. Today, the house, though it faces Canton Avenue, is closely bounded by Robbins Street on the left and Myers Lane in the rear, which leaves only a small front yard. It is a private residence. (Courtesy of the Milton Public Library.)

Harland Street once ran from Canton Avenue to Hillside Street and was a charming rural road lined with trees and stone walls. In the late 19th century, Unquety Road was laid out through the Blue Hills Reservation and bisected this street, effectively causing the end closest to Canton Avenue to become a dead end. Harland Street, as seen from Canton Avenue, has new houses that were built in the last four years on the site of the old Tucker-Miller Woodworking Mill and adjacent land. (Courtesy of the Milton Public Library.)

Looking west from Granite Place, seen on the right, one can see Adams Street, which was once known as the King's Highway and connected Boston to Plymouth Colony. In this 1905 photograph, the treelined street is primarily residential, but in the distance, the commercial stores in East Milton Square at Adams Street and Granite Avenue can be seen. On the right is the Gordon House, located at the corner of Granite Place, and the Adams House is just beyond that. (Courtesy of the Milton Historical Society, Whiting collection.)

Chapter 7
EAST MILTON

The Railway House was built in 1826 as a dining room and hotel for those visiting the Granite Railway Company operations in Railway Village, now known as East Milton. The building was also known as the Blue Bell Tavern, as guests and granite workers were summoned to hot meals by the ringing of a large blue bell on the property. Built of rough-hewn granite blocks, it stood on Adams Street between Edge Hill Road and Hollis Street. It is now the site of the Milton post office. (Courtesy of the Milton Public Library.)

The Charles H. Adams House was a duplex built in the 1830s, when the area was a thriving center for the dressing of granite quarried in Quincy. A large Greek Revival house, it was built at the corner of what is now Adams and Franklin Streets. A barbershop was located to the right of the house in the early 1900s. The house was demolished in 1917 to make way for a large commercial block on Adams Street in East Milton, and it is now the site of Video to Go. (Author's collection.)

The Babcock House was a Victorian Shingle-style house that stood near the corner of Granite Avenue and Adams Street. Adams Street became increasingly commercial after World War I, and many of the houses on the street were either demolished or moved to make way for the large commercial blocks that were being built in East Milton. This house was later moved to 2 Grafton Street at the corner of Edge Hill Road, where it was subdivided into a two-family dwelling. (Author's collection.)

The Glover-Adams-Gardner House was built *c.* 1785 at 594 Adams Street. A small cape, it was once the home of William N. Gardner, a master mason who, along with Joseph Coburn, laid the cornerstone of the Bunker Hill Monument in 1825, though it was presided over by the Marquis de Lafayette. One of the many houses that constituted Railway Village, it perpetuates the residential streetscape of Adams Street today. On the right is the Gordon House on the corner of Adams Street and Granite Place. (Courtesy of the Milton Public Library.)

The East Milton depot of the Granite branch of the Old Colony Railroad was built in 1872 at the corner of Adams Street and Granite Avenue. A train arriving from Boston approaches the depot as the traffic barriers are dropped in place. The Quincy Branch Railroad superceded the Granite Railway Company line, which ended in 1866. Later operated by the New York, New Haven and Hartford Railroad, the depot was closed in 1940, when the railroad ceased to operate. It was demolished in 1942. (Author's collection.)

The Hose No. 2 Engine House in East Milton was built at an angle between Adams Street and Granite Avenue in East Milton Square. On the left is Hodge's Drug Store, now the Rugby Building at 537 Adams Street, and on the right is the Sweerey House on Granite Avenue, which was later remodeled and became the Milton Cooperative Bank. The red-brick East Milton Fire House was built here in 1952. (Courtesy of Nadine Leary.)

The granite fountain located in front of the Hose No. 2 Engine House was given to the department in 1911 by Nathaniel Thayer Kidder (1860–1938), Milton's first tree warden and son of the co-founder of the investment firm Kidder Peabody and Company. Designed by Ludvig Sandoe Ipsen (1840–1920), it was a multipurpose dolphin-embossed fountain with a trough for horses, a drinking fountain for residents, and a low bowl for dogs. In 1942, the fountain was moved to Andrews Field, where it became a drinking fountain for children. On the right you can see a horse-drawn wagon near a string of boxcars on the railroad tracks. (Courtesy of the Milton Historical Society.)

East Milton Square was a bustling intersection *c.* 1905. A streetcar from Quincy can be seen entering the square via Bryant Street (Granite Avenue ran on the south parallel to the railroad tracks and Bryant Avenue on the north side), and horse-drawn wagons and automobiles travel along Adams Street. On the right is the Ellsworth Building, a large Colonial Revival commercial block that was owned by Henry E. Sheldon. Mullen Meat and Provisions, Charles E. Snow Dry Goods Store, and the J. J. Hammers Pharmacy were all located on the first floor. (Courtesy of Nadine Leary.)

The T. L. Pearce store was located at the corner of Adams and Church Streets. Three Milton residents lounge in front of the store *c.* 1895. An advertisement for O & O tea rests in the left window. Today, this is the site of Belle Visage. (Courtesy of the Milton Historical Society, Baxter collection.)

Charles Gallagher's Plumbing and Bicycle Repair Shop and the A. G. Coffin store were located on Adams Street (now the corner of Franklin Street). Today, Starbuck's coffee shop and Fleet Bank are located on the site, and on the far right can be seen the corner of the commercial block that is today the Milton (formerly Jim's) Barber Shop and Streamline Kitchen Design Center. On the left is now Franklin Street. (Author's collection.)

This *c.* 1945 northward view of East Milton Square from Granite Avenue show the commercial blocks that transformed this area between the two world wars into a distinctly profitable area. Notice the cars parked on the left, many of which were not only those of shoppers, but commuters who used the depot to commute to Boston via the Quincy branch of the Old Colony Railroad, later the New York, New Haven and Hartford Railroad. (Courtesy of the Milton Historical Society.)

In 1950, the square was photographed from the roof of the East Milton Fire House, showing the intersection of Adams Street and Granite Avenue. On the left is the Ellsworth Building, and on the right the Palisi Block. During the 1950s, the Southeast Expressway (Route 93) was constructed through this area as a suppressed six-lane highway with an overpass at Adams Street, which was known as the Babcock Underpass in honor of Rep. Josiah Babcock Jr. The Southeast Expressway opened to traffic in 1957, three years after the massive excavation began. In 1977, the overpass was redesigned as a community park and was named for M. Joseph Manning, a longtime and well-respected representative. (Courtesy of the Milton Public Library.)

Looking along Adams Street, this view shows the commercial streetscape of East Milton in the mid-20th century. Area businesses included Pendoley's Hardware, the Economy store, and the Hood Creamery. (Courtesy of the Milton Historical Society, Whiting collection.)

The Milton Cooperative Bank remodeled the first floor of this mid-19th-century house with a stone-veneer façade. The house is located on Granite Avenue adjacent to the East Milton Fire House. The Lewis and Son appliance store can be seen on the right. (Courtesy of the Milton Historical Society.)

The Milton post office was built by the English Construction Company between 1935 and 1937 on Adams Street, between Edge Hill Road and Hollis Street. It was designed as a Work Projects Administration building by Louis A. Simon, a federal supervising architect. The Colonial design was accentuated by the use of locally quarried granite laid in a random pattern with a distinctive wood louvered tower. The interior has a terrazzo floor with white-marble wainscoting and a fine historic mural painted by Elizabeth Tracy. (Courtesy of Nadine Leary.)

Kerrigan's Corner was named for Bernard Kerrigan (1850–1914), a well-respected town employee and the father of John F. Kerrigan, owner of the grocery store at the corner of Brook Road and Central Avenue. In this early-20th-century photograph, children stand under the canvas awning advertising Milton Spring ginger ale, with bottles in wooden boxes on the right. With cigars, confections, and a wide range of necessary items, Kerrigan's was a popular destination for decades for both shopping and socializing. (Courtesy of Bernadette C. Richards.)

Chapter 8
From Kerrigan's Corner to Cohan's Corner

A woman is seen waiting as a Wasson 10-bench open streetcar, on the far right, approaches Kerrigan's Corner (or Four Corners, as it was sometimes called) in this *c.* 1910 photograph. John F. Kerrigan (1888–1970) opened the store in 1903. He stands dressed in a white jacket in the doorway while patrons pose for the photographer. The front windows advertise Ferguson's breads and pies and White Seal bread. (Courtesy of Nadine Leary.)

The Cozzens-Baldwin-Cushing House was a large Greek Revival house built in 1838 at the corner of Canton Avenue and Reedsdale Road, opposite the Milton Public Library. Edward Baldwin enlarged the house and added fanciful Stick-style detailing in the Victorian period. The house was sold by the Cushing family and used as the parsonage of the First Congregational Church. In 1975, the large house was demolished, and the carriage house was converted into the present parsonage. (Courtesy of John Avery Tucker.)

The Touzalin-Pierce House was one of a number of large Shingle-style houses designed by William Ralph Emerson. The house was built for railroad magnate Edward A. Touzalin (1842–1890) on a large estate bounded by Canton Avenue, Highland Street, and Reedsdale Road. Known as Fair Oaks by Wallace Lincoln Pierce, it was his summer house; he kept a townhouse on Beacon Street in the Back Bay. In 1948, the estate was sold by the Pierce family, and the estate became the new site of the Milton Hospital, which was designed by Joseph Daniels Leland (1886–1968) of Leland and Larson and was built in 1950. (Author's collection.)

The transfer station of the Old Colony Street Railway, which provided trolley service through Milton, was a low, one-story wood-framed building located at 287 Reedsdale Road. It was adjacent to a four-bay carbarn, seen on the left. Commuters could wait, either on benches flanking the entrance or inside during inclement weather, for the streetcar that connected Lower Mills and Quincy, or a connecting streetcar to Randolph via Randolph Avenue. Today, 291 and 295 Reedsdale Road occupy the site of the carbarn, and the transfer station is a private residence. (Author's collection.)

Cohan's Corner is at the junction of Randolph Avenue (Route 28) and Pleasant Street. Named for Cornelius and Dermis C. Cohan, who kept a general store there for many years, it was located at the major intersection with Reedsdale Road. This watercolor by Kenney shows the traffic indicator on the left and a large Packard automobile stopped in front of the store. Today, Frame It Studio and Gallery and Tedeschi's Market are on the left, and what was a garage and gas station on the right is now an unpaved vacant lot. (Courtesy of Harriet Manning.)

This northward view from 1950 of the Blue Hills Parkway from Brook Road shows the dual roadway that had been laid out by the Olmstead Associates at the end of the 19th century. An alley of trees connected Mattapan Square and Canton Avenue, the entrance to the Blue Hills Reservation. Impressive houses were built on both sides of the new parkway that were uniformly set back and faced the green strip, thereby creating an attractive and well-designed neighborhood. (Courtesy of the Milton Historical Society, Hamilton collection.)

Chapter 9
Mattapan

The Cornell-Austin House, seen in 1875, was an impressive Greek Revival mansion that faced Mattapan Street (now the Blue Hills Parkway) and was located between Eliot Street and Brook Road. Set back from the street, it had a circular carriage drive with lavish horticultural plantings. The Honorable Arthur Austin was a founder of the town of West Roxbury in 1851 and moved to this house following the Civil War. Through his years here, he embellished the property and made it into a local showplace. In 1889, the house became the Boston Home for Aged and Infirm Hebrews and Orphanage, after which the area was developed as part of Briarfield, a residential development by Thomas S. Richardson and William G. Cruckshank. (Author's collection.)

The Hollingsworth-Russell House is at the corner of the Blue Hills Parkway and Curtis Street. This shaded scene shows Mattapan Street before it was redesigned in 1899 by the Olmstead Associates and renamed the Blue Hills Parkway. The house, at 42 Blue Hills Parkway, was built by Amor Hollingsworth and remodeled in the early 20th century by local architect and building inspector Fred N. Russell as his private residence. (Courtesy of the Milton Historical Society.)

The Jackson-McLean-Hollingsworth House was built *c.* 1712 on the Milton side of the Neponset River, close to the bridge that spanned the river. A large house, it was owned in the 19th century by Mark Hollingsworth (1777–1858), a partner with Edmund Pitt Tileston in the Tileston and Hollingsworth Paper Company. The noted artist George Hollingsworth (1813–1882) and his family lived here until the house was demolished in 1899. The grounds were incorporated into the protected green space that ran along the south bank of the Neponset River. Today, the Metropolitan District Commission station occupies the site. (Courtesy of the Milton Historical Society, Baxter collection.)

The Bartlett Block was an impressive commercial structure at the junction of the Blue Hills Parkway and Blue Hill Avenue. Built in 1899 by Jonathan B. L. Bartlett, it was a Queen Anne, Tudor Revival, red-brick commercial block with a rounded tower with a conical roof and a prominent clock in the front gable facing Mattapan Square. It was built adjacent to the owner's house at 75 Blue Hills Parkway. The Bartlett Block was demolished in the early 1970s, and today it is a small triangular garden. (Author's collection.)

The Blue Hills Parkway, seen in this bucolic photograph from 1955, shows the mature alley of elm trees that lined the center green space that ran from Mattapan to the entrance to the Blue Hills on Canton Avenue. The trees were laid out by the Olmstead Associates and created not just an impressive vista but an important entrance to the Blue Hills Reservation, which was laid out and designed by Charles Eliot, a noted landscape architect and local resident. The Blue Hills Parkway has seen the replanting of trees that have needed replacement, though their species and small stature cannot yet compare to the grace of the original plantings. (Courtesy of the Milton Public Library.)